School Daze

ALSO BY LOUIS PHILLIPS

How Do You Get a Horse out of the Bathtub?
Profound Answers to
Preposterous Questions

263 Brain Busters
Just How Smart Are You, Anyway?

Sportsathon
(with Vic Braden)

Haunted House Jokes

Going Ape
Jokes from the Jungle

How Do You Lift a Walrus with One Hand?
More Profound Answers to
Preposterous Questions

Way Out!
Jokes from Outer Space

Wackysaurus
Dinosaur Jokes

Invisible Oink
Pig Jokes

School Daze

Jokes Your Teacher Will Hate

by LOUIS PHILLIPS
illustrated by SUSANNA NATTI

VIKING

For Miranda Lucci

I hope this book proves to be

a help to you

when you start school.

—L. P.

VIKING
Published by the Penguin Group
Penguin Books USA Inc., 375 Hudson Street, New York, New York 10014, U.S.A.
Penguin Books Ltd, 27 Wrights Lane, London W8 5TZ, England
Penguin Books Australia Ltd, Ringwood, Victoria, Australia
Penguin Books Canada Ltd, 10 Alcorn Avenue, Toronto, Ontario, Canada M4V 3B2
Penguin Books (N.Z.) Ltd, 182–190 Wairau Road, Auckland 10, New Zealand

Penguin Books Ltd, Registered Offices: Harmondsworth, Middlesex, England

First published in 1994 by Viking, a division of Penguin Books USA Inc.

1 3 5 7 9 10 8 6 4 2

Library of Congress Cataloging-in-Publication Data

Phillips, Louis.
School daze : jokes your teacher will hate / by Louis Phillips ;
illustrated by Susanna Natti.   p.   cm.
ISBN 0-670-84929-4
1. Riddles, Juvenile. 2. Schools—Juvenile humor. I. Natti, Susanna. II. Title.
PN6371.5.P495 1994 818'.5402—dc20   93-41484 CIP AC

CONTENTS

No more school,
No more books,
No more teachers' dirty looks!
                    —Traditional chant

Row, row, row your boat
Gently down the stream.
Throw the teacher overboard,
Then you'll hear her scream!
                    —Traditional chant

CHAPTER ONE

Pre-K
or, Making Little Things Count

KINDERGARTEN CHILD #1: What are you doing?

KINDERGARTEN CHILD #2: I'm writing a letter to my little sister.

KINDERGARTEN CHILD #1: But you don't know how to write.

KINDERGARTEN CHILD #2: That's all right. My little sister doesn't know how to read.

TEACHER: Mary, do you know who in the Bible built the Ark?

MARY: No . . . ah . . .

TEACHER: Correct.

TEACHER: J.P., what is used to conduct electricity?

J.P.: Why . . . er . . .

TEACHER: Correct. Wire is often used to conduct electricity.

TEACHER: Bart Midwood, what is the basic unit for measuring power in a lightbulb?

BART: What?

TEACHER: Correct. The watt is the basic unit.

Is that dog on the couch again?

TEACHER: How do you spell *dog?*
JESSICA: D-O . . .
TEACHER: Well, what's at the end of it?
JESSICA: Its tail, of course.

MOTHER: How was your first day at school? Anything happen?
JESSICA: Naah. This old woman got up in front of the classroom and she didn't know how to spell *dog,* so I told her.

TEACHER: What do you call the outside of a tree, Herbert?
HERBERT: I don't know.
TEACHER: Bark.
HERBERT: All right, if you insist. *Woof, woof, woof!*

TEACHER: What do you call the outside of a cow, Herbert?
HERBERT: I don't know.
TEACHER: Hide. Hide, the cow's outside.
HERBERT: All right, if you insist. But I'm not afraid of any silly cow.

TEACHER: How do you spell *infinity?*
JOHN: I-N-F-I-N-I-T . . .
TEACHER: Well, what's at the end of it?
JOHN: It doesn't have an ending.

MRS. HOM: Nicholas, can you name two pronouns?
NICHOLAS: Who? Me?
MRS. HOM: Correct. Now, Perry Gold, what does
    W-H-A-T spell?
PERRY: What?
MRS. HOM: Correct. Now, Scott Cherry, can you
    give me an example of a sentence that asks a
    question?
SCOTT: Why are you asking me the tough one?
MRS. HOM: Correct. Now, Daniel Brawner, I would
    like an example of a compound sentence.
DANIEL: You might like one, but I'm not prepared.
MRS. HOM: Correct! Now, Annie Curley, can you
    give me an example of a complex sentence?
ANNIE: I can't give one, because I lost my home-
    work when my dog ate it.
MRS. HOM: Good. My, what an intelligent class!

TEACHER: What is the plural of goose?
SUE: Geese.
TEACHER: Correct. And what is the plural of child?
SUE: Twins.

TEACHER: If apples are three for a dollar, how many apples would you have if I gave you five dollars?
AMY: None.
TEACHER: None? How can you say none?
AMY: Because if you gave me five dollars, I'd go to the movies.

TEACHER: How much is one half of 8?
ROBERT BUTTERWORTH: Do you mean horizontally or vertically?
TEACHER: I don't understand. What do you mean?
ROBERT BUTTERWORTH: Well, 8 divided horizontally is 0, whereas 8 divided vertically is 3.

SCOTT: Do you know how to spell *banana?*
LUCAS: Yes, but once I get started spelling it, I never know when to stop.

TEACHER: Annette, can you spell *Philadelphia?*
ANNETTE: P-H-I-L-D-E-L-P-H-I.
TEACHER: What happened to the A's?
ANNETTE: They moved to Oakland.

SCIENCE TEACHER: Did you know that oxygen was
discovered in 1774?
OLIVIA KATZ: What did people breathe before then?

TEACHER: Who can use the word *diploma* in a sentence?
JASMINE: I can.
TEACHER: Go ahead, Jasmine.
JASMINE: When the sink got all clogged, we called
diploma.

MR. COLWELL: Who can name the poles of the earth?
CARTER: I can: North, South, and Tad.

TEACHER: Nancy, how many feet are there in a yard?

NANCY: I guess it depends how many children are playing in it.

Jennifer came home right after her first day of school. Her mother asked her,

MOTHER: What did you learn today, dear?

JENNIFER: Not enough. I have to go back tomorrow.

OLIVIA KATZ: Let's play school.

ANDREW KATZ: Okay. Today I'm absent.

MRS. CHISHOLM: Who can use the word *column* in a sentence? Helen Cherry, can you?

HELEN: Yes, ma'am: When I can't visit my friends in person, I column up on the phone.

TEACHER: Which is closer—the moon or Russia?

ALBERT: The moon.

TEACHER: Why do you say that?

ALBERT: Because at night I can see the moon, but I can never see Russia.

GEOGRAPHY TEACHER: I would like to point out that the Hudson River was discovered by a man named Henry Hudson.
RORY: Isn't that a remarkable coincidence!

TEACHER: Don, how much is 3 plus 5?
DON: Eight.
TEACHER: Very good.
DON: Very good? Are you kidding? It's perfect.

TEACHER: Tony, stop acting like an idiot.
TONY: Who's acting?

MOTHER: How did things go in school today?
GINNY: Oh, the teacher showed a movie, and the students all stood up and walked out.
MOTHER: That's terrible. Why did they do that?
GINNY: The movie was over.

BOB: That new girl in school—where is she from?
KAY: Alaska.
BOB: Don't bother. I'll ask her myself.

TEACHER: Can someone please tell me one use for cowhide?
MICHAEL MALLORY: Well, it holds the cow together.

TEACHER: What did Noah say just before he entered the Ark?
MATTHEW: Now I *herd* everything.

LEO BOOKMAN: What did your teacher say about your homework?
CHARLIE: I didn't do it.
LEO BOOKMAN: Well, how did the teacher respond to that?
CHARLIE: He took it like a lamb.
LEO BOOKMAN: What do you mean?
CHARLIE: He looked at me and said "Baaa!"

MRS. BOYKINS: Today we shall be learning about the weather. What does it mean when the barometer falls?
PERRY GOLD: Whoever nailed it up didn't do a very good job.

LORNA: Why did the kindergarten teacher wear sunglasses to class?
LESLIE: I don't know. Why?
LORNA: Because her pupils were so bright.

TEACHER: Ryan, did you do your arithmetic lesson?
RYAN HOFFMAN: Yes, ma'am. I added up that column of figures ten times.
TEACHER: Very good.
RYAN HOFFMAN: Thank you. Here are my ten answers.

TEACHER: Suppose you had two dollars in one pocket of your pants and a twenty-dollar bill in the other. What would you have?
IAN: Somebody else's pants.

TEACHER: All right, suppose you had five dollars and you asked your father for ten dollars. What would you have?

IAN: Five dollars.

TEACHER: No you wouldn't.

IAN: Yes I would. You don't know my father.

TEACHER: If 3 plus 3 is 6, and 6 plus 6 is 12, how much is 12 plus 12?

WENDY: That's not fair!

TEACHER: Why not?

WENDY: You answered the easy ones and left the hard one for me.

PETER: I'm the teacher's pet.

IAN: How come?

PETER: Because she can't afford a dog.

TEACHER: There will be an eclipse of the moon tonight. Perhaps your parents will let you stay up and watch it.

GEORGE: What channel will it be on?

TEACHER: Albert, what is the first letter of the name *Yellowstone?*
ALBERT: Y.
TEACHER: Because I asked you, that's why.

KINDERGARTEN CHILD: Hey, Mom, I won a prize in school today.
MOTHER: That's wonderful. How did you do it?
KINDERGARTEN CHILD: The teacher asked how many legs a kangaroo has, and I guessed three.
MOTHER: Three? How could you possibly win a prize with that answer?
KINDERGARTEN CHILD: My answer came the closest.

MOTHER: Well, Luke, how are you doing in your wood-carving class?
LUKE: Oh, I'm getting better, whittle by whittle.

DANIEL B.: I'm going to take banjo lessons.
MATTHEW: Good. Go home and stop picking on *me.*

TEACHER: Annie, what do you like best about your home?

ANNIE: From my bed, I can see the sun rise.

TEACHER: And Oona, what do you like best about your home?

OONA: From my bed, I can see the kitchen sink.

TEACHER *(holding up a picture)*: Who can identify this bird?

DENNIS KRAMER: That's a gulp.

TEACHER: A gulp? There's no such bird as a gulp.

DENNIS KRAMER: Yes there is. It's just like a swallow, only larger and louder.

TEACHER *(holding up a chart of bird pictures)*: Leila, can you name five of these birds?

LEILA: Yes I can. I name them Amy, John, Andy, Don, and Pat.

TEACHER: Lauren, why are you laughing up your sleeve?

LAUREN: Didn't you say that's where my funny bone is?

TEACHER *(to a kindergartner)*: Katrina, go up to the map, please, and show us where America is.

KATRINA: Here it is.

TEACHER: Very good. Now class, can you tell me who discovered America?

KINDERGARTEN CLASS: Katrina just did.

TEACHER: Where were you born, Tobey?

TOBEY: South America.

TEACHER: What part?

TOBEY: All of me, of course.

CHAPTER TWO

First Through Sixth Grade
or, Elementary, My Dear Watson!

TEACHER: Alex, if I had two sandwiches and you had two sandwiches, what would we have?
ALEX: Lunch!

TEACHER: Harley, you don't look too well today. How do you feel?
HARLEY: Well, I have a slight cold.
TEACHER: Do you have a temperature?
HARLEY: Not anymore. The school nurse took it.

TEACHER: Now class, who memorized a poem for today? Yes, Harry?
HARRY: Roses are red,
Violets are blue.
If a skunk went to college
It would go to P. U.

LESLIE: How do you like your third-grade teacher?
LORNA: She's a peach.
LESLIE: You mean she's sweet?
LORNA: No. I mean she has a heart of stone.

TEACHER: I have ten apples in my left hand and twelve apples in my right hand. Amy, what do I have?
AMY: Huge hands.

TEACHER: Please, Amy. Pay attention. Now, I have thirteen potato chips in my left hand and fourteen potato chips in my right hand. What do I have?
AMY: Greasy palms.

BIOLOGY TEACHER: Can someone identify this tree?
NANCY: It's a dogwood tree.
BIOLOGY TEACHER: How can you tell?
NANCY: By its bark.

TEACHER: Can you name something you grow in your garden?
MELVIN: Tired.

After Agnes, a third grader, had finished her book report about a mystery story, the teacher said, "That was a very good book report, and I am pleased that you didn't give away the ending to the class."

"Well," Agnes said, "if they really want to know the ending, they can rent the video themselves."

TEACHER: Susan, I am disappointed in the results of your history test. When I was your age, I knew the names of all the presidents.
SUSAN: Yes, but there were so few presidents then.

TEACHER: Can someone give me an example of wasted energy?
DELIA: Telling a hair-raising story to a bald-headed person?

BIOLOGY TEACHER: Tiffany, what do we call the last teeth a human being gets?
TIFFANY: False.

DANIEL: I'm glad that I'm named Daniel.

HALEY: Why?

DANIEL: Because that's what everybody calls me.

TEACHER: George, what is the shape of the world?

GEORGE: Seems terrible to me.

TEACHER: Be serious. What is the shape of the world?

GEORGE: I don't know.

TEACHER: Well, what shape are the earrings your mother wears?

GEORGE: Square.

TEACHER: Does she have any in other shapes?

GEORGE: She wears round ones on weekends.

TEACHER: Very good. So then what is the shape of the world?

GEORGE: I know. Round on weekends and square on weekdays.

TEACHER: If a baby eagle is called an eaglet, what do we call a baby owl?

KEN HOLMES: A hootentot?

TEACHER: Kaitlin, what was George
Washington most famous for?
KAITLIN: His memory?
TEACHER: His memory? How
can you say that?
KAITLIN: Because in Washington,
D.C., there is a monument to
Washington's memory.

JOSHUA: Can I call you sometime to ask about the
homework?
GILLIAN: Anytime.
JOSHUA: What's your phone number?
GILLIAN: It's in the phone book.
JOSHUA: What's your last name?
GILLIAN: Oh, that's in the phone book too.

JOHN: Teacher, what part of the body is the *fray?*
TEACHER: What are you talking about?
JOHN: Well, it says right here in our history text
that a Confederate general was shot right in the
thick of the fray.

TEACHER: Alex, can you tell the class where the English Channel is?
ALEX: I don't know. We don't have cable, so we don't get it on our TV.

KAY: What book are you reading for school?
JENNIFER: It's really good. It's called *How to Pay Attention When People Talk to You.*
KAY: Who wrote it?
JENNIFER: Excuse me, what did you say?

TEACHER: Scott, can you tell me the definition of *zero?*
SCOTT: Nothing to it.

MRS. BOYKINS: Patricia, I am curious about something you wrote in this essay.
PATRICIA: What is it?
MRS. BOYKINS: Why do you say that the citizens of New York are noted for their stupidity?
PATRICIA: Well, in the encyclopedia it says that the population of New York City is extremely dense.

GINNY: What are you taking up in school?
JOHN: Space.

TEACHER *(to a first grader on her first day of school)*: Suzy, you look unhappy. Are you homesick?
SUZY: No, I'm here sick.

TEACHER: Diane, what important historical event happened in 1809?
DIANE: Abraham Lincoln was born.
TEACHER: Good. Now tell me what important historical event took place in 1812.
DIANE: Lincoln celebrated his third birthday.

MRS. COTTAM: What are you going to study when you get out of school?
BEN: I want to be a barber.
MRS. COTTAM: How long will that take you?
BEN: Not long. I'll take shortcuts.

TEACHER: Charlie, can you tell me another name
for the Dog Star?
CHARLIE: Are you Sirius?

SUNDAY SCHOOL TEACHER: Are there any questions?
CHARLIE BOOKMAN: Is it true that human beings
are made from dust?
SUNDAY SCHOOL TEACHER: That's what it says in
the Bible.
CHARLIE BOOKMAN: And is it true that after they
die humans turn back to dust?
SUNDAY SCHOOL TEACHER: That is what it says in
the Bible.
CHARLIE BOOKMAN: Well, I looked under my bed
this morning, and someone's either coming or
going.

RACHEL: Tell me, Chaim, were the test questions
easy?
CHAIM: The questions were easy enough. It was
coming up with the answers that was hard.

DR. MARKOE: Why were there fewer accidents before the invention of the automobile?
NANCY: Because back in horse-and-buggy time, the
drivers didn't depend entirely upon their own in-
telligence.

MR. KARMON: Today we are going to have lessons in first aid. Joseph, what would you do if you broke your arm in two places?
JOSEPH: I wouldn't go to those two places anymore.

SCHOOL NURSE: Your cough sounds much better this morning.
ALBERT: It should. I've been practicing all night.

MS. REGENT: Ian, please use the word *acquire* in a sentence.
IAN: My brother wanted to sing Handel's *Messiah,* so he found a place in acquire.

RYAN HOFFMAN *(doing his math homework)*: Dad,
how do you find the lowest common denominator?
FATHER: Are they still looking for that thing?
Teachers were looking for it when I was in school.

SCIENCE TEACHER: Corey, could you please tell the
class what happens when a body is fully sub-
merged in water?
COREY: Yes, teacher. As soon as a body is fully sub-
merged in water, the telephone rings.

MRS. BRUCK: Could you please use the word *centimeter* in a sentence?
SPENCER: My sister was late coming home from
school, so I was centimeter.

PETER: What's the difference between a school-
teacher and a railroad train?
IAN: What?
PETER: A train is a *choo choo,* while a teacher
makes you spit out your gum so you can't *chew
chew.*

TEACHER: Do you realize that every second I breathe, someone dies?
DEBORAH: Did you ever try mouthwash?

MRS. TURLEY: What is the chemical formula for water?
LAUREN: H, I, J, K, L, M, N, O.
MRS. TURLEY: That's a strange answer.
LAUREN: Why? Didn't you say the other day that the chemical formula for water was H to O?

MS. REGENT: Now that you have read the story of Tom Sawyer, can anybody describe how he laughed?
IAN: Huck . . . Huck . . . Huck . . .

MS. REGENT: What are geologists?
IAN: Music lovers.
MS. REGENT: What do you mean by that?
IAN: Don't they dig rock?

MRS. COTTAM: Ben, what are *thongs?*
BEN: Thongs are what Frank Thinatra things.

MRS. BOYKINS: What are the last words of "The
Star Spangled Banner"?
MATTHEW: Play ball!

MRS. TURLEY: Nancy, could you please tell the class
what you know about the Second Amendment to
the Constitution?
NANCY: Certainly. The Second Amendment is the
one that says we can pull up our sleeves.
MRS. TURLEY: That's a strange answer.
NANCY: Why? Doesn't it say that we have the right
to bare arms?

MRS. PINTO: Does anyone in this class know where
the Great Plains are located?
MATTHEW: Kennedy Airport?

MRS. BIRCHILL: Daniel, could you please use the word *budget* in a sentence?
DANIEL: I wanted to move my desk to the other side of the room, but I couldn't budget.

MRS. HOFMAN: Did *Great Expectations* have a happy ending?
RYAN: Yes. Everyone in the class was glad when it was over.

MRS. BOYKINS: Spencer, could you please use the word *windows* in a sentence?
SPENCER: First prize in the contest is two tickets to a basketball game. I hope I windows.

TEACHER: The only way to get ahead in life is to start at the bottom and work your way to the top.
ALEX BREEN: But I want to be a deep-sea diver.

ENGLISH TEACHER: How many *i*'s do you need to spell *Mississippi?*
PETER MARTIN: None. I can spell it blindfolded.

CHAPTER THREE

Junior High and Beyond

or, Several Degrees of Humor

TEACHER: Leila, can you tell me something about the Dead Sea?

LEILA: Dead Sea? I didn't even know it was sick!

TEACHER: What do you know about Czechoslovakia?

LEILA: Hard to say.

MAX: First I got tonsillitis, followed by appendicitis and pneumonia, ending up with neuritis. Then they gave me hypodermics and inoculations.

BEN: Did you miss a lot of school?

MAX: No. I'm talking about my spelling test.

TEACHER: Could you close the window, Natalie? It's cold outside.

NATALIE: If I close the window, will it be warm outside?

TEACHER: Can someone tell me a ten-letter word that starts with G-A-S?

PAUL: Automobile?

TEACHER: What's the tallest building in the world?
JOANNE: The Library of Congress.
TEACHER: Why the Library of Congress?
JOANNE: Because it has the most stories.

HISTORY TEACHER: Matthew Wasserman, can you
recite Lincoln's Gettysburg Address?
MATTHEW: I'd be happy to. Lincoln's Gettysburg
address was 314 Sharpwell Lane.

MS. WHITAKER: Can anyone choose a year and tell
me the number of television sets found in Ameri-
can homes at that time? Yes, Eliza?
ELIZA VALK: 1910. Zero sets.

Did you hear about the cannibal who was expelled
from school for buttering up the teacher?

In the school library, several junior-high-school students were acting up and being very noisy. "Please be quiet," the librarian asked. "The other students here can't read."

"Then what are they doing in here?" a student asked.

TEACHER: Carol, can you name nine animals found in India?

CAROL: Eight tigers and a water buffalo.

MRS. GREENE: Paul, why aren't you sketching with the rest of the class?

PAUL: I ain't got no pencil.

MRS. GREENE: Please don't say, "I ain't got no pencil."

PAUL: Yes, ma'am.

MRS. GREENE: You have no pencil. I have no pencil. She has no pencil. We have no pencils.

PAUL: Gee! Who's stealing all the pencils around here?

BIOLOGY TEACHER: Albert, what would you do if you had rabies?

ALBERT: The first thing I would do is get a sheet of paper and a pencil.

BIOLOGY TEACHER: A sheet of paper and a pencil? Why would you do that?

ALBERT: To make a list of all the people I want to bite.

KAI: Teacher, you know the question you asked us yesterday?

TEACHER: Where does the sun go when it goes down?

KAI: That's the one.

TEACHER: What about it?

KAI: My brother Eric and I stayed up all night trying to figure out the answer.

TEACHER: And did you and your brother solve the problem?

KAI: Well, the answer finally dawned on us.

TEACHER: Ivan Johnson, where was the Declaration of Independence signed?
IVAN: At the bottom, of course.

A teacher in high school was administering a true-or-false test, and she watched in astonishment as a student in the very front row started tossing a coin into the air. The student would flip the coin and then make a mark on his test paper.

"Why are you doing that?" the teacher asked.

"Oh, I'm just using the coin to determine the answers," the student said. "If the nickel comes up heads, the answer is True. If it comes up tails, the answer is False."

The student did all fifty questions that way. Then, after finishing the test, the student started to flip the coin again.

"What are you doing now?" the teacher asked.

"Checking my answers," was the reply.

CHAPTER FOUR

A Short Recess

TEACHER *(in the school yard)*: Is this your handball, Matthew?

MATTHEW: Are there any broken windows?

TEACHER: Not as far as I know.

MATTHEW: Then that's my handball.

After a summer spent at the beach, Susie returned to school badly burned and peeling. As she walked across the playground, another young girl looked at her and said, "Oh, look at poor Susie. She's only five years old and she's already wearing out."

P.E. INSTRUCTOR: Deborah, can you stand on your head?

DEBORAH: Of course not. I can't step that high.

JOAN: What are they serving in the school cafeteria today?

KAREN: Oh, a hundred things.

JOAN: What are they?

KAREN: Beans.

JOHN: I don't like this school.
AMY: Why not?
JOHN: Because it's haunted.
AMY: What makes you think that?
JOHN: Because the teacher keeps talking about
school spirit.

On the first day of school after summer vacation, two
students met on the playground.
TED: Hey, Danny, you've changed a lot. Before the
summer, you were really overweight, and now
you're skinny.
JOE: My name is Joe, not Danny.
TED: Wow! You've changed your name, too!

COLIN: What are you going to bring to class for
show-and-tell?
MIRANDA: I'm going to bring my surgeon doll.
COLIN: What does your surgeon doll do?
MIRANDA: It operates on batteries.

TEACHER: Joanna, what happened to you during recess? You're a mess.
JOANNA: I fell into a puddle.
TEACHER: In your brand-new dress?
JOANNA: I didn't have time to change.

TEACHER: In the Bible, it says that Lot's wife looked back and turned into a pillar of salt.
GENE HURLEY: That's nothing.
TEACHER: What do you mean, that's nothing?
GENE HURLEY: Why, just the other day, my uncle was out driving, and he looked back and turned into a telephone pole.

P.E. TEACHER: I hope you children do a lot of swimming over the summer, because swimming is a good exercise to keep thin.
LESLIE: How come it doesn't work for whales?

ELIZABETH: What's the difference between an engineer and a teacher?

SPENCER: That's what I say. What's the difference?

ELIZABETH: No. Come on. What's the difference between an engineer and a teacher?

SPENCER: What?

ELIZABETH: One minds the train while the other trains the mind.

ROGER: Boy, is Sarah smart. She got 100 on her math test. She has brains enough for two.

LOUIS: Then she's just the girl for you.

DAVID: Dillon, are you tan from the sun?

DILLON: No. I'm Jones from the earth.

TEACHER: Today I am going to show a film. Are the blinds drawn?

JUEL: No, they're real.

TEACHER *(on the playground)*: Roy, why are you
making faces at me?

ROY: I'm sorry, teacher. It's just that I don't feel
well.

TEACHER: What's the matter?

ROY: My head feels like a piece of iron, my neck is
as stiff as a pipe, and my muscles are like steel
bands. Do you think we should call for the school
nurse?

TEACHER: It sounds like we should call for a
plumber.

STEVEN: How do you like your new teacher?

IVY: I don't.

STEVEN: Why not?

IVY: When I went to school this morning, she said,
"Sit up front for the present."

STEVEN: What's wrong with that?

IVY: She didn't give me any present.

MRS. FROSCH: Danny, can you please complete this famous proverb: Early to bed and early to rise makes a man . . . what?
DANNY: An expert at making breakfast?

SCOTT JEFFRIES: Did you take math this semester?
IAN: No. Is it missing?

MOTHER: Scott, what happened at school today?
SCOTT: Dennis broke a window.
MOTHER: Dennis broke a window? How did that happen?
SCOTT: I threw a rock at him and he ducked.

MOTHER: Did someone at school give you that black eye?
DENNIS: Are you kidding? I had to fight for it.

LORNA: Are you going to study any languages this year?

LESLIE: Why should I? I know every language in the world, except Greek.

LORNA: Do you know Chinese and Russian?

LESLIE: They're all Greek to me.

DORIS: May Bob and me go to the cafeteria?

ENGLISH TEACHER: May Bob and *I* go to the cafeteria.

DORIS: Okay. You can go with Bob if you really want to.

LESLIE: What have you been doing in school lately?

LORNA: I have a part in the school play.

LESLIE: Great! What's the name of the play?

LORNA: *Delicatessen.*

LESLIE: And do you have a big role?

LORNA: No, but I have a loaf of rye bread and some biscuits.

MARVIN: How was science class?
SARAH: Great. We discovered an acid that will dissolve everything. It's a shame, though.
MARVIN: Why do you say that?
SARAH: Because we can't find anything to put it in.

TEACHER: Can anyone here spell *Tennessee?*
SCOTT KRAMER: One-essee, two-essee, three-essee, four-essee . . .

Blake is sitting at a lunch table with his teacher.
BLAKE: Could you please pass the nuts?
TEACHER: Not unless they do their lessons correctly.

RYAN HOFFMAN: Will you tutor me in history?
LOUIS: I'll be glad to, but I charge fifty cents for every two questions you want answered.
RYAN HOFFMAN: Isn't that awfully expensive?
LOUIS: Yes it is. What is your second question?

LUKE: Hey, Mom, I got 100 today!
MOM: That's marvelous. What did you get 100 in?
LUKE: Three subjects: a 30 in math, a 20 in history, and a 50 in English.

ORRI: What's the matter?
RONI: I have to choose between taking an art class and P.E.
ORRI: Gee, that's a tough choice.
RONI: Yes, it is. What would you do if you were in my shoes?
ORRI: Polish them.

NORMAN: I wonder what I should be after I graduate.
ELMER: I think I'll be a chimney sweep.
NORMAN: Soot yourself.

TEACHER: I hope you punished your son for mimicking me.
FATHER: Of course I did.
TEACHER: Good!
FATHER: I told him not to act like a fool.

MOTHER: How do you like school, Mildred?
MILDRED: Closed.

TEACHER: Who invented spaghetti?
ORRI: I did!
TEACHER: Why did you say that?
ORRI: I don't know. It just popped into my noodle.

JOANNE: What book are you doing your report on?
KAY: *Fannie Farmer's Cookbook.*
JOANNE: *Fannie Farmer's Cookbook?* Why are you doing a report on a cookbook?
KAY: Because it has so many stirring chapters in it.

JOHN: I think the teacher is trying to make a monkey out of me.

AMY: Why should she take all the credit?

ANGELA: Have you completed your science report about the moon?

KATE: Yes, I have.

ANGELA: What do you say about it?

KATE: I say it's going broke.

ANGELA: How can the moon go broke?

KATE: Well, I just heard on the news that it was down to its last quarter.

JOHN: Did the photographer take your school picture?

AMY: He did, but I don't think the pictures do me justice.

JOHN: It's not justice you want, it's mercy!

CHAPTER FIVE

Excuses! Excuses! and More Excuses!

MRS. CARLSON: Jon, why are you late?
JON: I guess it's because class started before I got here.

TEACHER: Amanda, why are you so late for class this morning?
AMANDA: I fell over fifty feet.
TEACHER: You fell over fifty feet? And you didn't get hurt?
AMANDA: No. I was just walking through a crowded bus.

TEACHER: Katherine, why are you late for school?
KATHERINE: I burned my finger in hot water.
TEACHER: You should have felt the water before you put your hand in.

TEACHER: Ian, your essay called "Our Turtle" is word for word the same one your brother Matthew wrote on the subject. How do you explain that?
IAN: Easy. Same turtle.

TEACHER: Shannon, I hope I didn't see you copying
those answers from Mary's paper!
SHANNON: I hope you didn't, too!

JONATHAN: I studied history for four hours last
night and I still flunked the test.
ROSS: Do you have any idea why?
JONATHAN: I guess it was because the test was on
math.

MRS. FARINA: Ian, you're late for school again.
What's your excuse this time?
IAN: I was having a dream about my Little League
game.
MRS. FARINA: And so?
IAN: My team was at bat and the game was tied.
MRS. FARINA: But why are you late?
IAN: Because the game went into extra innings, and
I couldn't wake up until it was my turn to bat!

TEACHER: Teddy, why are you late for school?
TEDDY: I twisted my foot.
TEACHER: Sounds like a lame excuse to me.

TEACHER: Matthew, did you miss school yesterday?
MATTHEW: No, not at all.

MRS. HOLM: Jessica, why did you come to school dripping wet?
JESSICA: It's not my fault. I was brought to school in a car pool.

JAMES: Teacher, would you punish someone for something they didn't do?
TEACHER: Of course not. You know I wouldn't.
JAMES: Good. Because I didn't do my homework.

BOBBY: What do you have to pay to go to school?
RYAN: Attention.

MICHAEL: I'm sorry, teacher. I is late for class.
TEACHER: "I is late for class." What has happened to your grammar?
MICHAEL: Nothing. She's safe at home, as far as I know.

TEACHER: Miranda, why are you crawling into class on your stomach five minutes late?
MIRANDA: Because of what you said.
TEACHER: What did I say?
MIRANDA: You told me never to walk into class late again.

TEACHER: Amy, why are you so late for school every morning?
AMY: Oh, because of that stupid sign.
TEACHER: What stupid sign?
AMY: The one that says, SCHOOL AHEAD. GO SLOW.

TEACHER: Patricia, every morning you are late to school. Why is that?
PATRICIA: Because you're always ringing the bell before I get here.

JOHN *(on the phone)*: I am calling to tell you that John is not feeling well and cannot come to school today.
PRINCIPAL: Who is this?
JOHN: My father.

TEACHER: Orri, why are you so late for school?

ORRI: My mother's in the hospital.

TEACHER: Oh, I'm so sorry.

ORRI: That's all right. She's a nurse.

TEACHER: Why are you late for school?

ELIZABETH BERGER: Because of the explosion.

TEACHER: What explosion?

ELIZABETH BERGER: Didn't you hear it?

TEACHER: No, I didn't.

ELIZABETH BERGER: Well, just a few minutes ago, the wind blew up the street.

FATHER: Were you late for school yesterday?

ESMERALDA: Yes, I was, but it doesn't matter.

FATHER: What do you mean it doesn't matter?

ESMERALDA: Well, don't you say all the time that it's never too late to learn?

CHAPTER SIX

Report-Card Time

TEACHER: What is it, Sandy?

SANDY: I don't want to scare you, but my father said if I don't get better grades on my next report card, somebody's going to get spanked.

SEAMUS: I don't think I deserve a zero on this test.

TEACHER: Neither do I, but it's the lowest grade I could give you.

PETER MARTIN: Dad, can you write in the dark?

DAD: Certainly.

PETER MARTIN: Good. Then can you turn off the lights and sign my report card?

BRIDGET: Here is my report card. I hope you realize that Joan of Arc and I have a lot in common.

MOTHER: What do you have in common?

BRIDGET: We both went down in history.

MOTHER: Nancy, why is your January report card filled with C's and D's?

NANCY: Well, you know how it is, Mom. Things are always marked down right after Christmas.

ALBERT: Here's my report card. And here's another one.

FATHER: What's this second report card?

ALBERT: It's one I found in the attic. It's your fifth-grade report card. See? Your failing grades are exactly the same as mine.

FATHER: Is that so?

ALBERT: That's so.

FATHER: Then I guess, to be absolutely fair, I'll have to give you what my father gave me!

FATHER: Sam, come here.

SAM: Yes, Father.

FATHER: What's the meaning of the D and F on your report card?

SAM: That means "Doing Fine."

IVY: Why did you get an F in history?

STEVEN: It's not my fault.

IVY: Why not?

STEVEN: The teacher's always asking me about things that happened before I was born.

MOTHER: What do these 0's on your report card mean?
MELISSA: It's the moon. The teacher ran out of stars.

TEACHER: Can anyone tell me where the Red Sea is located?
DIANE: I can. It's on the third line of my report card.

TEACHER: Spencer, do you think ordinary paper can keep people warm?
SPENCER: I sure do. The last report card I took home kept my father hot under the collar for a week.

FATHER: Tell me, Henry, why did you fail history?
HENRY: I just don't understand it. Everything the history teacher says goes in both ears and out the other.
FATHER: But that's three ears!
HENRY: I'm not doing very well in arithmetic either.

COLIN: My mother can tell the future with cards.
MIRANDA: Is she a fortune-teller?
COLIN: No. She can take one look at my report card and then predict what will happen to me when my father gets home.

HISTORY TEACHER: When did the Great Depression take place?
AGNES: After I brought home my report card.

PETER: Hey, Dad, you're going to be happy.
DAD: Why?
PETER: Because I'm going to help you save money.
DAD: How are you going to do that?
PETER: Well, you remember you said you would give me ten dollars if I got good grades on my report card?
DAD: Yes, I do.
PETER: Well, today's your lucky day. You don't have to pay me.

FATHER: Don, I don't understand why you are doing so badly in arithmetic.

DON: Well, it's because on Monday, the teacher said 2 plus 6 equals 8.

FATHER: So?

DON: Well, then on Tuesday, she said 4 plus 4 equals 8.

FATHER: So?

DON: Then on Wednesday, she said 5 plus 3 equals 8.

FATHER: So?

DON: How do you expect me to do well in arithmetic if the teacher can't make up her mind?

MOTHER: I can't stand how expensive everything is getting. Everything is going up. The price of food is going up. The price of clothes is going up. The landlord is going to raise the rent. I would be happy if I just knew of one thing that went down.

RONI ADA DRUKS: Then be happy, Mom. Here's my report card.